To: Peter

To remind him of his youth

Bristol

2016

NORTH-EAST ENGLAND

Graeme Peacock

CONTENTS

MYRIAD

LONDON

North Northumberland coast

Beautiful beaches and magnificent castles abound in this region –
the birthplace of Christianity in England.

The north coast of Northumberland is a mix of vast empty beaches and characterful coastal villages. The area is dotted with mighty castles such as Dunstanburgh and Bamburgh – a testament to the fact that the region experienced centuries of warfare between the Scots and the English. This area is also the "cradle of English Christianity" with the beautiful holy island of Lindisfarne at its heart.

BERWICK Trapped inside the Elizabethan walls of 1596 that enclose the town, much of Berwick-upon-Tweed's ancient street pattern still survives. Parts of Edward I's castle can still be seen, with its famous White Wall descending down the hill towards the river like some medieval staircase. In this violent period the town changed hands between England and Scotland 13 times before finally surrendering to the English in 1482. The old harbour that played such an important part in the history of Berwick is still to be seen with the wealthy merchants' houses and doorways to their cellars cut through the walls. Just upstream, with its arches reflected in the water, is the long narrow Old Bridge; its 15 arches were built between 1611 and 1624. The bridge carried the Great North Road until 1928 when the Royal Tweed Bridge with its four massive spans of reinforced concrete was built to improve the flow of traffic. The Royal Border Bridge, also known as the Railway Bridge, was designed by Robert Stephenson and built between 1847-1850. In the surrounding countryside small villages such as Etal, with its thatched pub and houses with unusually large roof slates, still fascinate the visitor.

BAMBURGH CASTLE

Perched on its huge rock Bamburgh Castle can be seen for miles around; it dominates the pretty village below, clustered around its wooded green. The churchyard has a monument to Grace Darling together with the graves of victims of shipwrecks on the nearby Farne Islands.

The first known fortification here was a wooden palisade built around 547, although the site had been occupied since the Iron Age. The castle's name comes from that of Bebba, the wife of Ethelfrith who ruled Northumbria from 593 to 616, and it soon became known as Bebbanburgh. Its huge Norman keep has walls some 11ft (3m) thick; the building we see today is a combination of restoration by Lord Crewe, Bishop of Durham in the 18th century, and then later by the first Lord Armstrong, the Victorian industrialist. Standing on the shoreline and looking up to the castle it is easy to see why it is such a favourite with film directors.

LINDISFARNE CASTLE, HOLY ISLAND The posts that stand in front of Lindisfarne Castle on Holy Island are the remains of a jetty where lime was loaded onto ships bound for Dundee in the 1870s. Further evidence of this trade can be found in the huge limekilns still standing beneath the castle. Built around the year 1550 from stones robbed from the nearby priory, the castle was designed to offer protection to the harbour, which had become a strategic naval base guarding against possible raids by the Scots. It saw action during the Civil War and was briefly captured by two supporters of the Scottish cause in 1715. Even though it continued to be garrisoned it gradually declined and was last used by an artillery detachment in the 1860s after which it began to fall into disrepair. In 1902 the castle was bought by Edward Hudson, the founder of *Country Life* magazine. He employed Sir Edwin Lutyens to restore the building and convert it into a home. In 1944 the castle was given to the National Trust.

ST CUTHBERT'S ISLE To the west of Holy Island is the small rocky outcrop known as Cuthbert's Isle. St Cuthbert had a small hermitage and chapel here around 670; a short walk across the rock pools at low tide brings you to the site of the chapel marked by a large cross. Some 500 years later St Cuthbert's successors built the magnificent arch of the west doorway to the priory that clearly bears the hallmarks of its Norman builders.

BIRTH OF CHRISTIANITY The bronze statue of St Aidan stands on the edge of the village of Lindisfarne. The monastery Aidan founded in 635 became a great seat of learning and the Lindisfarne *Gospels* were produced here. In 793 the monastery was destroyed by the Vikings. By 1132 a priory had been founded and it is the ruins of this building we see today. The threat of invasion was so great that the priory was built with stone battlements.

THE FARNE ISLANDS The Farne Islands are owned by the National Trust and consist of a group of islands 2.5 miles (4km) off the fishing village of Seahouses; between 15 and 28 islands are visible depending on the state of the tide. The islands form one of Britain's most important seabird sanctuaries. The closest island is Inner Farne and the furthest out, at 4.4 miles (7km) from the shore, is Knivestone. The chapel on Inner Farne is built on the site of St Cuthbert's Oratory. It was from the Longstone lighthouse situated on one of the outer Farne islands that Grace Darling and her father rowed out to rescue the survivors of the ship-wrecked *Forfarshire*. The lighthouse was built between 1825 and 1826.

Often referred to as "Europe's Galapagos", the Farnes have over 50,000 pairs of nesting puffins and an additional 48,000 pairs of other species.

SEAHOUSES Tourist boats and fishing vessels sit side by side in Seahouses harbour. Seahouses grew out of the village of North Sunderland when the fishermen built the "sea houses" by the side of the harbour. For a while the village was known by the name of North Sunderland Sea-Houses. The flat roof behind the old limekilns betrays the fact that a railway bringing the raw materials once terminated on top of it. The lime industry flourished up until the 1850s when the fishing industry took over, fuelled by the demand for herring – the demand was so great that in 1834 over 6,000 barrels of salted herring were dispatched to the Baltic States and Germany. As a result, a new harbour was built at a cost of £25,000, opening in June 1889.

BEADNELL The sun sets over the small boats or *cobles* nestling in the harbour of Beadnell. This fishing port is very unusual: despite the fact that it is on the east coast, the harbour was built so it can only be entered by boats approaching from the west. In the late 1700s the huge sweep of Beadnell Bay was popular for horse-racing and at the time the village was well known as a centre for smuggling. The beach at Beadnell is capped at its northern end by the harbour and limekilns. Dating from 1789 these huge kilns were last used for lime production in the 1820s; later they were used for herring curing. In the summer up to 60 local fishermen worked the keel boats operating out of the harbour often accompanied by boats from Cornwall and Scotland. Today, Beadnell is not only a working fishing village but also one of the most popular holiday beaches in the region. Fierce storms breached the harbour wall during a bad storm in 1997.

DUNSTANBURGH Today the most notable feature of Dunstanburgh Castle is the Lilburn Tower, clearly visible for miles around. Dating from 1323 the ground floor of the castle would have held provisions while the upper floor provided accommodation. Dunstanburgh's strategic importance can easily be seen from the vantage point of her towers. Looking south towards the small village of Craster the coast sweeps southwards towards Newton and Howick eventually arriving at Alnmouth, Amble and Coquet Island. In the early 1380s major alterations were carried out by John of Gaunt. Among these are the stark remains of the great gatehouse that, unusually, doubled as a keep; this still conveys the power of this wonderful building.

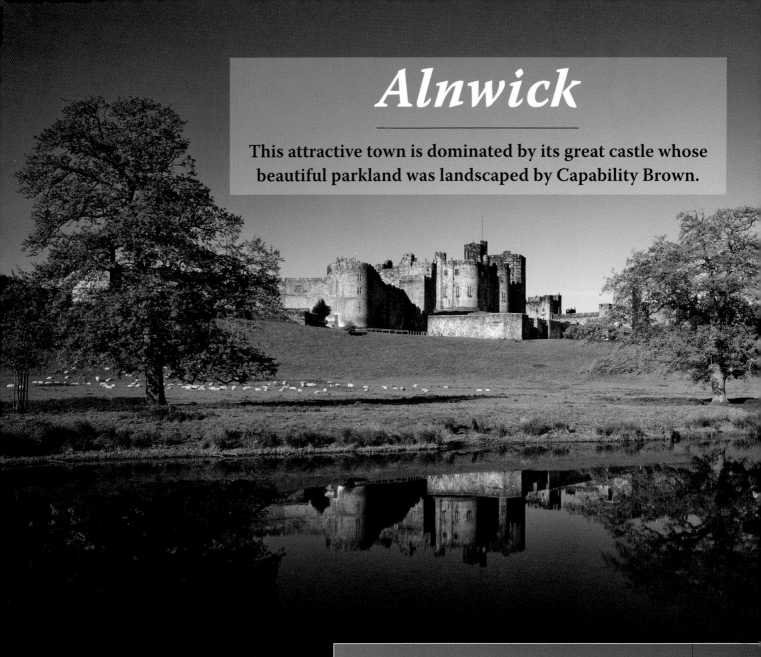

Alnwick

This attractive town is dominated by its great castle whose beautiful parkland was landscaped by Capability Brown.

Often called the Windsor of the North, the rolling fields and scattered copses betray the hand of the famous landscape gardener Capability Brown who laid out Alnwick's grounds in the 18th century. The 14th-century barbican at Alnwick is one of the most impressive in the country. Built as a motte and bailey castle by the Normans it was acquired by the de Vescys in 1090 and in 1309 passed into the hands of the Percys. The castle was restored in the 19th century and today the walls look over the river Aln and the park below. The lion of the Percy family stares at all who drive into the town from the north and gives the bridge its name. Every Shrove Tuesday Alnwick's two parishes play each other in a unique game of football, a centuries old tradition.

CASTLE FILMS Alnwick Castle is often used as a location for films and television programmes; two block-busting movies – *Harry Potter and the Philosopher's Stone* and *Harry Potter and the Chamber of Secrets* were filmed here. The castle also appeared in the first series of the popular television comedy *Blackadder*. In 2010 it was seen in Ridley Scott's *Robin Hood* starring Russell Crowe.

ALNWICK CASTLE
The centre of Alnwick Castle consists of a large, fortified block set around a small courtyard containing the most important rooms. The imposing walls which surround the castle are dotted with large towers at various intervals and these are used today to house special exhibitions. About one-sixth of the outer wall has been removed over the centuries.

ALNWICK GARDEN AND TREEHOUSE Enclosed by walls which are 250 years old, Alnwick Garden is believed to be one of the largest walled gardens in the world. On entering the visitor is greeted by the Grand Cascade where 7,260 gallons of water per minute tumble down 27 weirs, disappearing into four large bell mouth openings, to reappear at the other side of a walkway in four "mounds" of water. The three large central jets reach a height of 20ft (6m), with 40 smaller jets sending water 15ft (5m) into the air. These are complemented by 80 side jets that create sweeping curves of water to the centre of the Cascade. Outside the walls of the main garden is one of the world's largest wooden treehouses, an enormous structure of turret-topped buildings and amazing walkways in the sky that link the different sections. The site on which Alnwick garden is built has had a colourful history, with gardens being planted here by leading contemporary designers.

ALNWICK MARKETPLACE The marketplace in Alnwick has long been a meeting place for the people of the town; it dates back to the 1200s. With its cafes, shops, cobbled surface and market cross the area forms the ideal location for the town's music festivals and craft and farmers' markets. The buildings that surround the square are varied in their age and architecture; the town hall, built in 1771, is not owned by the council but by the "freemen of Alnwick". Standing some 83ft (25m) high the fine fluted stone Tenantry Column has an internal staircase leading to a gallery at the top. It was raised in 1816 by grateful tenants of the Duke of Northumberland, who reduced their rents after the Napoleonic wars to alleviate their hardship. The Duke then decided that if they could afford such a gesture they could afford the rents and he promptly raised them again. Thus the column is known locally as the "Farmers' Folly".

ALNMOUTH CROSS

Alnmouth is a sleepy little village at the mouth of the river Aln. Founded in 1150 as a medieval borough, in 1207 the village was granted a charter for a port and a market. By the 18th century the main export was grain and many of the granaries can still be seen, now converted into houses. Imports into Alnwick included slates, timber and guano. A giant wooden cross on the southern side of the Aln estuary marks the site of the original village church of Alnmouth. In 1806 a great storm blew up which forced the Aln to change course and cut the church off from the village. The storm also made access into the port by large vessels almost impossible and so destroyed much of Alnwick's sea-borne trade.

Northumberland

A sparsely populated region dotted with mighty castles, fortified houses and attractive villages.

BELSAY HALL AND CASTLE Sir Charles Monck was greatly influenced by the art and culture of the ancient Greeks. In 1817 he decided to build a Grecian-style house on his estate at Belsay and employed some of the finest craftsmen of the day to do so. Belsay Hall has one of the most beautiful and fascinating gardens in Northumberland. It is full of corridors, arches and ravines with vines, ferns, palms and exotic and rare plants. In the late 19th and early 20th centuries Sir Charles' grandson Sir Arthur Middleton extended the garden and introduced rhododendrons and other plants new to the country at the time.

In the grounds of the estate is the original Belsay Castle, a conglomeration of building styles completed down through the ages. The original castle was a tower house built around 1360 which still has its battlements and arrow vents. In the early 17th century a two-storied range was built alongside and in 1717 a further wing was added although little remains of this extension today.

CHILLINGHAM The large cannons that sit outside Chillingham Castle bear witness to the violent past of one of Northumberland's most fascinating castles. Now a stately home open to the public, Chillingham Castle has seen more than its fair share of border warfare and is reputed to be one of the most haunted houses in the county. Amongst the ghosts is Lady Mary Berkeley; it is said that her rustling dress can still be heard along the corridors and stairs accompanied by a chilling blast of air. The present structure dates from 1344 when Sir Thomas Grey built a courtyard and curtain wall around an old pele tower. In 1590 the main entrance was moved to its present position, in preparation for the visit of King James VI of Scotland on his journey south to London for his coronation.

AMBLE HARBOUR In the days when Amble was a thriving port the sailors from the various countries who traded here called it "the friendliest port" due to the hospitality they received. Officially known as Warkworth harbour, Amble harbour was constructed in 1839 and owes its existence to its coal exports. Although one of Northumberland's most important fishing ports, Amble today also has an excellent yacht marina and is renowned for leisure sailing. Compared to other ports Amble still has a large fishing fleet and is regarded as a traditional working port. Boatbuilding has always been carried on in the town and it continues to this day. The larger fishing boats that moor along the harbour wall land a variety of fish, crabs, lobsters and prawns and working cobles can still be seen in the inner harbour.

BLYTH BEACH To the north and south of Blyth's harbour entrance are wide open beaches. Much of the coastline to the north consists of sand dunes with their typical grasses and habitats. Like other ports in Northumberland, Blyth owes its present size to the development of the coal industry, reaching its peak in the 1960s. Nowadays large wind vanes can be seen on the harbour wall supplying electricity. This row of nine 300kw Windmaster turbines generates green electricity. At the time, the turbines were the largest erected offshore in the world. In the middle ages the beaches either side of the estuary were sited next to saltpans which provided the town with a thriving trade. Today Blyth is a bustling, modern port. The town is also well-known for its "Lighthouse in the street". It was built in 1788 by Sir Matthew White Ridley who owned Cowpen Colliery and had his own wharf at the harbour. Then, the lighthouse stood only 10 yards from the sea wall but continuous development over the years has resulted in it now being positioned in a back lane.

MORPETH The river Wansbeck flows sedately through Morpeth, one of the major market towns of Northumberland. The footbridge shown here is actually built on the abutments and central piers of the medieval bridge that crossed the river and was destroyed in 1832. By the side of the main bridge, built by Thomas Telford in 1831, is a block of buildings that are relics of the 13th-century chantry chapel of All Saints where tolls were collected and which was also a school. It was attended by William Turner (1508-1568), the "Father of English Botany". Little remains of the castle as it was burnt by King John and virtually destroyed in the Civil War. Emily Davison, the suffragette killed by the king's horse in the 1913 Derby, is buried near to the castle. Admiral Collingwood, Nelson's second-in-command at Trafalgar, hailed from Morpeth; his home can be seen in Oldgate Street.

WARKWORTH CASTLE Built on a mound on a loop of the river Coquet, Warkworth was originally a wooden fortress built after the Norman Conquest. During the Middle Ages the wooden structure was gradually replaced by strong stone battlements; the imposing keep was added in the 14th century. The Percy family who owned the castle sided with the northern earls who took up arms against Elizabeth I. Thomas Percy, 7th Earl of Northumberland, was executed in 1572 and Warkworth slowly fell into disrepair.

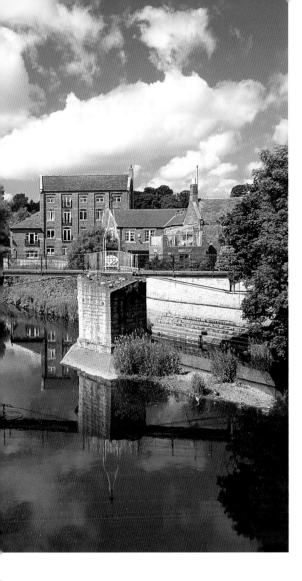

WALLINGTON HALL Unlike other great houses in Northumberland, Wallington is sited close to a main road on the other side of which is the walled garden. The four magnificent stone griffin heads which sit at the roadside are said to have adorned one of London's original mediaeval gateways. A castle which was once owned by the famous Fenwick family of Northumberland once stood here and the present house is sited on its cellars. A square house was built on top of a Tudor mansion when Sir John Fenwick sold it to Sir William Blackett in 1688. Work began on the present house in 1783 by Sir Walter Calverly Blackett. In 1846 Sir Walter Trevelyan inherited it; the extensive gardens were landscaped by local man Lancelot "Capability Brown", the famous landscape gardener who was born at nearby Kirkharle.

CAMBO Set back from the main road, Cambo has an air of tranquillity. The village consists of a group of terraced cottages enclosing a square with a walled green and several well-stocked, attractive private walled gardens. Cambo was first laid out as a model village in 1740. An early chapel dating from the 12th to the 15th centuries was demolished in 1875, but a few coffin lids were preserved and are now set into the walls of the present church which was consecrated in 1842 and built by Sir John Trevelyan, the owner of Wallington Hall; several members of the Trevelyan family are buried in the churchyard. The old schoolhouse (left) which was altered and enlarged in 1911, had Capability Brown as one of its pupils.

Border Country

This is the site of Hadrian's Wall, the most heavily fortified border in the Roman Empire. In later years the region was much fought over by the English and the Scots.

Hadrian's Wall was begun in AD122 and eventually stretched 73.5 miles (117km) from Wallsend on the river Tyne to the shores of the Solway Firth. A great deal of the middle section of the wall is largely intact and along its length are the ruins of a number of forts and milecastles. The well-preserved ruins of the fort at Housesteads (above) show how the Romans made use of the steep slopes of the escarpment at Whin Sill as a major defensive element in the construction and siting of the wall.

HOUSESTEADS Built when the Roman Empire was at its height, Housesteads is the best-preserved example of a Roman fort in the country. It held a garrison of around 1,000 men, most of whom were German auxiliaries. Unlike other forts along the

BIRDOSWALD This is one of the most spectacular locations of any fort on the Roman wall as it stands on a high spur of land overlooking the Irthing Gorge. Parts of the original turf wall built in AD122 can still be clearly seen. A small museum on site illustrates the lives of the soldiers who were stationed at this unfriendly outpost of empire. The stone from Hadrian's Wall was looted over the centuries and used for other buildings in nearby towns and farms, resulting in the piecemeal structure we can see today. The Romans also reduced the width of the wall, using fewer stones as they progressed westwards.

wall, Housesteads is built on quite a noticeable slope; the Romans sited their granaries on the highest part of the fort to keep the food inside dry. By the 13th century, Housesteads became a hiding place for reivers (cross-border raiders) and the cattle they had stolen.

FORTS AND WATCHTOWERS
Hadrian's Wall is part of an overall defensive system consisting of forts and watchtowers. In this part of Northumberland the Roman fort of Vindolanda was used to accommodate the local Roman soldiers. Amongst the many tablets found on the site are requests for warm woollen clothing to be sent to the legionaries from home. These notes are remarkably similar to the letters sent home from soldiers in the trenches in the First World War.

SYCAMORE GAP The lone sycamore tree standing in a prominent position on Hadrian's Wall close to Steel Rigg gives the name to this well-known beauty spot, north of the A69 between Haltwhistle and Haydon Bridge. Sycamore Gap became famous when it was used as a location for scenes in the 1991 movie *Robin Hood: Prince of Thieves*, which starred Kevin Costner. The tree is 70 years old; in the film a great deal of work was needed to turn it into an English oak similar to those found in Sherwood Forest.

KIELDER WATER The largest artificial lake in Europe, Kielder Water holds a staggering 200 billion litres of water and supplies the people and the industries of the north-east. Kielder Castle was built in 1775 as a shooting lodge for the Duke of Northumberland and now acts as the main visitor centre for the park, which has become a centre for recreational activities such as sailing, canoeing, cycling and birdwatching. The reservoir is surrounded by the vast Kielder Forest, the largest planted forest in Europe. The main species of tree in the forest is Sitka spruce; this hardy tree survives well in this hostile upland environment.

FONTBURN RESERVOIR Situated ten miles north-west of Morpeth at the southern edge of the Cheviot Hills, Fontburn Reservoir was constructed at the end of the 19th century to provide water for the surrounding areas of south-east Northumberland.

LINHOPE SPOUT This dramatic 50ft (15m) high waterfall is in the Breamish Valley a few miles to the west of Powburn. It lies on the Linhope Burn, a tributary of the river Breamish. The waterfall lands in a plunge pool 6ft (2m) wide and 16ft (5m) deep. The best time to visit is in midsummer, preferably after a long spell of rain. Well-marked paths lead up to the waterfall from the village of Linhope which lies about a mile south-east of the Spout.

HEXHAM ABBEY There has been a church on this site for over 1300 years. In 674, Wilfrid, Bishop of York, who was educated at Lindisfarne, established a Benedictine abbey here. In 875 the building was largely destroyed by the Vikings and it was not until about 1050 that a church was rebuilt on the site. This in turn was replaced in the early 13th century by an Augustinian priory and it is this church, built in the early English style, that we see today. The Saxon crypt and apse is all that remains of Wilfrid's original abbey. Since the Dissolution, the abbey has been used as the parish church of Hexham.

CORBRIDGE The countryside around Corbridge is noted for its beauty and the town's parks and riverside walks are popular. The Northumberland Show is held annually in the fields outside the town and draws visitors and exhibitors from all over the county. One of the most important supply depots for Hadrian's Wall was at Corbridge just north of the present town. It occupied a strategic position at the point where the Stanegate, the road running parallel with the wall towards Carlisle, met Dere Street, the main road into Scotland where it crossed the Tyne. Much of the stone from the site was used to build Hexham Abbey and parts of Corbridge itself. The bridge at Corbridge was built in 1674 and is still the main route into one of Northumberland's most interesting towns. It was so well built that it was the only bridge on the Tyne to withstand the great flood of 1771 when it was said the water was so high that people could lean over the parapet and wash their hands. Corbridge is known for its quaint town centre and individual shops and is an ideal base from which to explore beautiful Northumberland.

BREAMISH VALLEY This remote and wild valley is situated on the eastern edge of the Northumberland National Park with the tiny settlement of Ingram at its heart. The village itself consists of a small scattering of houses dominated by the Cheviot Hills to the west. The river Breamish passes along the northern edge of the village. The valley is dotted with Neolithic and Bronze-Age settlements, making this one of the most important archaeological landscapes in Britain.

CHEVIOT HILLS These rolling hills straddle the Scottish-English border and stretch across the northern half of Northumberland ending in the valley of the river Coquet. The hills are criss-crossed by bridleways, many marking the routes of ancient cattle-droving routes used in the past both by herdsmen taking their animals to market and by smugglers and raiders to move cattle and other contraband materials in seclusion. Today these paths are used by walkers or mountain bikers. The highest point in Northumberland, Cheviot Summit, is south of Kirk Yetholm close to the Scottish border. The wild flat summit stands at a height of 2674ft (815m). The Pennine Way long-distance footpath snakes along the border ridge close by. The National Park Centre at Ingram in the Breamish valley contains information on walking and sites of interest in the southern Cheviots.

ELSDON The Vicar's pele tower at Elsdon was built about 1400. The village also has the spectacular remains of a Norman motte and bailey castle and is noted for its large sloping green and the nearby Winter's Gibbet. One of the rectors here was Charles Dodgson who, from 1762 to 1765, was a tutor to the Duke of Northumberland's son. He was also the great grandfather of Lewis Carroll, the author of *Alice in Wonderland*. The village is noted for its massive motte and bailey castle built by Robert d'Umfraville in the 11th century. The Battle of Otterburn was fought close by and some of the dead are buried under Elsdon Church.

YEAVERING BELL HILL FORT The largest Iron Age hill fort in the region, Yeavering Bell lies on the edge of the Cheviots some three miles north of Wooler, enclosing some 13 acres. Its most remarkable feature is the preservation of a massive stone-walled rampart, in places some 12ft (4m) wide, which encloses much of the summit and can be easily seen from the roads below. Inside the fort are traces of 130 hut platforms. Beyond the main wall which encloses all of the summit are additional defensive stone outworks on the east and west sides. An entire town existed here 2,000 years ago until it was abandoned sometime around the 1st century. It is not clear why but the walls do appear to have been deliberately flattened which suggests that the Romans may have destroyed the fort. After the Roman withdrawal, the fort remained in use until the reign of King Edwin in the 7th century.

CRAGSIDE With its mixture of German, French and Old English styles Cragside has a majestic appearance and is surrounded by a 1000-acre forest garden. In fact, with its hot and cold running water, fire alarms, central heating, telephones and a Turkish bath it was known as "The Palace of the Magician". Home to William Armstrong, the north-east's leading industrialist of his day, the house was begun in 1869 and finished in 1884. It was the first house in the world to be lit and powered by hydroelectricity. Lakes were created to make stunning vistas and azaleas and rhododendrons planted to give the astounding displays for which the estate is famous. Over 7 million trees and bushes were planted and hundreds of boulders were manhandled into position to create a fantastic rock garden with tumbling waterfalls and scenic views from bridges and paths.

COQUETDALE The beautiful Coquetdale has a timeless air about it; with its bracken and rocky outcrops it is easy to imagine the valley's earliest human inhabitants carving the many cup and ring mark patterns, and horsemen driving stolen cattle along the river's edge. Harbottle dominates the valley and is home to the castle where Margaret, Countess of Lennox, grandmother of James VI of Scotland and I of England, was born. The valley offers stunning scenery all year round and is part of the Northumberland National Park. A few miles up the valley, where the Coquet meets the Alwin, is Alwinton, now famous for its Border Shepherds show, the last of the many agricultural shows that are held throughout the region. Heading north out of the village is Clennel Street, one of the great droving roads that heads northwards to the border.

SIMONSIDE HILLS Lying within the Northumberland National Park, these hills are formed from a dramatic sandstone escarpment. They offer easy walking with fine views especially in the northern sector overlooking Rothbury where the famous Lordenshaws hill fort can be found.

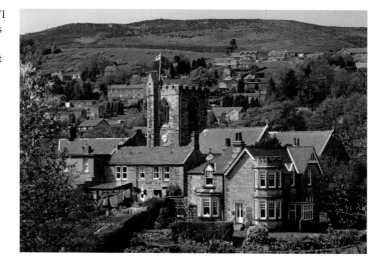

ROTHBURY With its sloping green shaded by sycamores, Rothbury is known as the capital of Coquetdale. The Anglo-Saxons had a royal burgh here and the town was an ancient barony passing through various owners before coming into the hands of the Percy family in the 1330s. Rectors from the church can be traced back to 1107 and in 1291 Edward I granted a charter for a Thursday market and an annual fair.

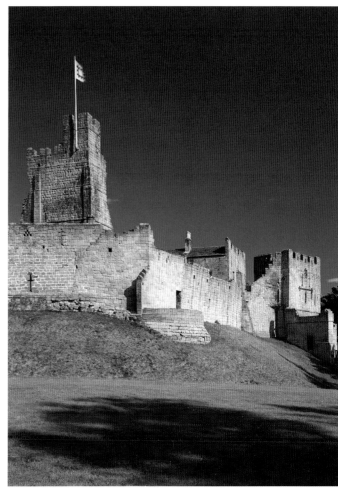

PRUDHOE CASTLE The name Prudhoe means "proud hill". The castle which lies on the south bank of the Tyne is protected on the east by a steep ravine and is partly enclosed by a deep moat. It is first mentioned in 1173 when it was besieged by the Scots shortly after it was built by Odinel d'Umfreville. William the Lion of Scotland besieged the castle again one year later. The castle remained a fortress of the Umfrevilles until 1381 when it passed to the Percys. By the 19th century it had fallen into disuse and is now in the care of English Heritage.

LANGLEY CASTLE This elegant structure looks much as it did when it was first built in 1364. It was the stronghold of the Lucy family but after only 50 years it was gutted by fire. Since that time the castle has been a fortress, a private house, a barracks during the Second World War and a girls' public school. It is now a hotel.

North Tyneside

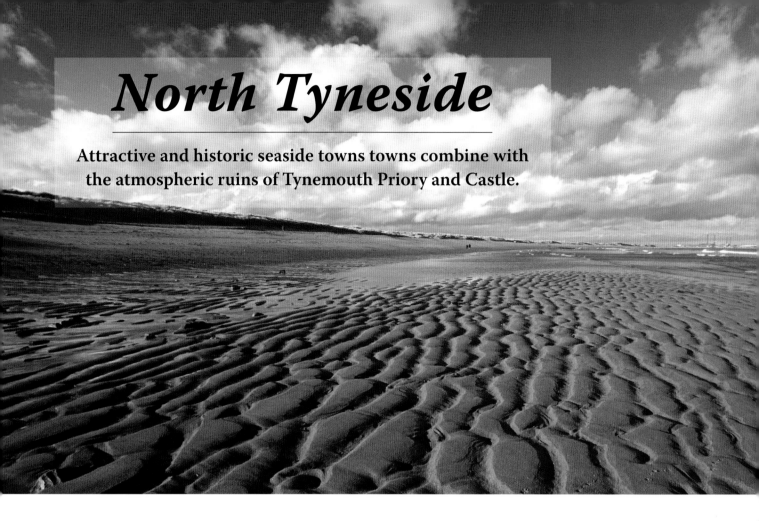

Attractive and historic seaside towns towns combine with the atmospheric ruins of Tynemouth Priory and Castle.

Nrth Tyneside is bounded by Newcastle to the west, the river Tyne to the south and Northumberland to the north. Historically, the area lies within the county of Northumberland and formed the south-easterly tip of this historic region. Since 1974 this varied area has been part of the metropolitan county of Tyne and Wear, which stands between the more industrial and populated city of Newcastle to the west and the North Sea. Its seaside towns and villages include North Shields, Whitley Bay, Cullercoats and Seaton Sluice all of which have a proud and colourful history as fishing and industrial ports, whilst Tynemouth is a busy market and fishing port as well as a seaside resort. Prominent on the headland close to the town are the ruins of Tynemouth Priory and Castle overlooking the mouth of the Tyne.

SEATON SLUICE SANDS To the north of the harbour of Seaton Sluice is an area of dunes and a long sandy beach. The sand dunes cover an area called Hartley Links which forms a protective barrier between the sea and the land. There have been attempts to protect this fragile environment by planting marram grass to help bind the dunes and stabilise them. This is a wonderful area in which to walk and enjoy views of the harbour and beach.

SEATON SLUICE Lying at the very southern border of the Northumberland coastline at the mouth of Seaton Burn, Seaton Sluice is made up of two separate villages, Seaton Sluice and Old Hartley; over the years they have gradually merged into one village. In the 17th century the mouth of Seaton Burn was treacherous and awkward for craft wanting to use the port. To alleviate the problem, in 1660 Sir Ralph Delaval built a stone pier to create a harbour. In 1690 Sir Ralph added sluice gates which closed as the incoming tide filled the harbour. At low tide the sluice gates were opened and a powerful flood of water flushed the harbour clean thus giving the port its name of Seaton Sluice.

SEATON DELAVAL HALL Built between 1719 and 1732 for Admiral George Delaval, Seaton Delaval Hall is regarded as the masterpiece of the celebrated architect Sir John Vanburgh, who also built Blenheim Palace and Castle Howard. This elegant English Baroque villa with its splendid gardens was gutted by fire in 1822; the interior state rooms remain largely unrestored since that time.

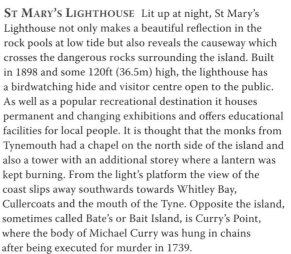

ST MARY'S LIGHTHOUSE Lit up at night, St Mary's Lighthouse not only makes a beautiful reflection in the rock pools at low tide but also reveals the causeway which crosses the dangerous rocks surrounding the island. Built in 1898 and some 120ft (36.5m) high, the lighthouse has a birdwatching hide and visitor centre open to the public. As well as a popular recreational destination it houses permanent and changing exhibitions and offers educational facilities for local people. It is thought that the monks from Tynemouth had a chapel on the north side of the island and also a tower with an additional storey where a lantern was kept burning. From the light's platform the view of the coast slips away southwards towards Whitley Bay, Cullercoats and the mouth of the Tyne. Opposite the island, sometimes called Bate's or Bait Island, is Curry's Point, where the body of Michael Curry was hung in chains after being executed for murder in 1739.

CULLERCOATS The lifeboat station at Cullercoats must be one of the most colourfully decorated in the country. The lifeboat was established here in 1852 and the boat today is an inshore inflatable lifeboat that can reach 32 knots. Cullercoats was originally a small fishing village and at one point had 15 cobles operating from the port; salt was also exported from here and it is recorded that the *Fortune of Whitby* sailed in July 1726 with 21 tons on board. Today the beach is very popular with Tynesiders and the Dove Marine Laboratory, an important facility for marine science, is sited here. Cullercoats was particularly popular with artists in the later years of the 19th century and work by the "Cullercoats Group" is now sought after by collectors. The American artist Winslow Homer spent two years in the town in the late 19th century producing many famous watercolours.

TYNEMOUTH PRIORY Perched on a clifftop, Tynemouth Priory is protected both by the sea and Tynemouth Castle, and is one of the largest fortified sites in the country. Originally the site was occupied by a 7th-century Saxon church, renowned as the burial place of St Oswin, king and martyr. The early monastery was sacked by the Danes in 800. The present buildings date from 1085 when a group of Benedictine monks from the abbey at St Albans arrived here; the monastery was finally completed at the end of the 13th century. The monks amassed great wealth from the coal industry which they used to finance the building work.

LONGSANDS This beach is popular with those wanting to bathe, surf or simply relax. Nearby is a park, sealife centre, toy museum and shops, making it an ideal seaside destination. The cliffs at Tynemouth offer an excellent vantage point from which to watch ships entering the Tyne estuary, especially when magnificent sailing ships call at Newcastle in the annual Tall Ships Race.

TYNEMOUTH CASTLE The massive gatehouse at Tynemouth Castle is an extension of the fortifications of the priory. The first castle here was a motte and bailey affair with a wooden palisade. The middle ages saw the castle act as a place of sanctuary. Charles I strengthened its defences and during the Civil War it was besieged and captured by both Royalist and Parliamentary forces. During the Second World War the castle was used as the base for a coastal defence unit.

NORTH SHIELDS The fish quay at North Shields with its distinctive lighthouse is one of the best-known views in the north-east. Although much diminished from earlier days, fishing is still important here. Today the town remains an important commercial centre and the modern Royal Quays shopping centre attracts thousands of shoppers. North Shields had its share of tragedy during the Second World War: in 1941 a bomb from a lone German raider scored a hit on the air raid shelter of the Wilkinson Lemonade factory killing 105 people. To the south is the Souter Lighthouse and the Whitburn Coastal Park; to the north is the Leas – two and a half miles of cliffs, beaches and grassland with spectacular views.

Newcastle & Gateshead

This exciting urban area has a rich industrial past and an unequalled heritage of fine architecture. Gateshead is home to The Sage and the Baltic Centre.

TYNE CROSSINGS The Tyne bridges hold a special place in the history of the north-east as they have performed a vitally important role in the region's social and economic development throughout the ages. Each of the bridges has its own story to tell. The Swing Bridge opened in 1876 and was specially designed to allow large ships to pass upriver. The High Level Bridge, which opened in 1850, is one of the most important structures in the history of the British railway system. Robert Stephenson's bridge brought Newcastle into the London-Edinburgh railway link and confirmed the East Coast line as the major rail route between the two cities. Opened by King George V in 1928 the Tyne Bridge is now associated with the swarming mass of runners crossing it as part of the Great North Run.

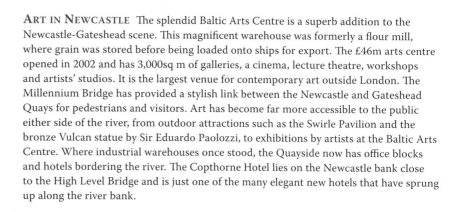

ART IN NEWCASTLE The splendid Baltic Arts Centre is a superb addition to the Newcastle-Gateshead scene. This magnificent warehouse was formerly a flour mill, where grain was stored before being loaded onto ships for export. The £46m arts centre opened in 2002 and has 3,000sq m of galleries, a cinema, lecture theatre, workshops and artists' studios. It is the largest venue for contemporary art outside London. The Millennium Bridge has provided a stylish link between the Newcastle and Gateshead Quays for pedestrians and visitors. Art has become far more accessible to the public either side of the river, from outdoor attractions such as the Swirle Pavilion and the bronze Vulcan statue by Sir Eduardo Paolozzi, to exhibitions by artists at the Baltic Arts Centre. Where industrial warehouses once stood, the Quayside now has office blocks and hotels bordering the river. The Copthorne Hotel lies on the Newcastle bank close to the High Level Bridge and is just one of the many elegant new hotels that have sprung up along the river bank.

MILLENNIUM BRIDGE AT NIGHT The lighting beneath the pedestrian deck of the Gateshead Millennium Bridge is seen here reflected on the surface of the slow-moving river Tyne. The arch is lit with a series of high-powered lights which change colour, the display blending in seamlessly with the buildings of Newcastle and Gateshead on either bank. The bridge creates a circular promenade in conjunction with the Swing Bridge that allows people to enjoy and appreciate both of the newly revitalised banks of the river. This walk is especially popular at night when separate sections are illuminated in different colours. Amazingly the bridge can be raised and lowered, silently, in only four minutes. When open, it allows ships 82ft (25m) headroom, the same as the clearance of the Tyne Bridge. When closed the clearance is 15.5ft (4.7m) and the navigation channel is 98.5ft (30m) wide, equal to that of the neighbouring Armstrong Swing Bridge.

THE SAGE The Sage Gateshead is a centre for music and the performing arts. The dramatic glass and stainless steel building on the south Quayside was designed by Sir Norman Foster and has been likened to a "resting armadillo". It has a 1,700 seat hall plus a flexible 450-seat auditorium and the interior of the building with its innovative walkways, stairs and brilliant lighting is a superb example of modern architecture. Around the front and sides of the Sage is a glazed concourse that provides stunning views of the Quayside and river. The roof of this incredible building holds over 3,500sq m of glass; this allows light to flood the building during the day and provides a colourful spectacle when the building is viewed from outside after dark.

CASTLE KEEP The keep is all that remains today of the "new castle" that gave the city its name. It was constructed as part of the rebuilding in stone of the castle carried out by Henry II and took 10 years to complete. Even today, this imposing structure gives an impression of immense military power. Newcastle Corporation supplied cannons to the keep to be fired on ceremonial occasions. This ended in tragedy in 1812 when one of the cannons exploded and a gunner was blown over the parapet. Next to the keep is the Black Gate, which dates back to before 1649. The slots which held the counterweights of the drawbridge are still clearly visible. Today, it is difficult to imagine that in the 19th century the Black Gate contained a pub, The Two Bulls' Heads and shops, and was home to more than one hundred people. By 1855 the building had become a tenement used as a centre for secondhand shoe and clothes dealers. The Castle Keep and Black Gate are now Grade 1 listed monuments; they are open every day for visitors.

CIVIC CENTRE Bathed in a blue light that seems to represent the waters of the Tyne, Newcastle's Civic Centre reflects much of the history and culture of this great city. Twelve seahorse heads cast in bronze, part of Newcastle's coat of arms, adorn the top of the tower. The heads are approximately 5ft (1.5m) in diameter. Sixteen feet (5m) up the exterior wall is a sandstone statue of the river god, with water pouring out of his outstretched hand. This imposing building has three wings arranged round a courtyard and a 12-storey main block to the north, capped by a copper lantern and beacon and a circular debating chamber to the west. King Olaf of Norway officially opened the Civic Centre in 1968. The city's links with the countries of Scandinavia are symbolised by the bronze statue of swans soaring into flight in the courtyard. The dramatic Law, Business and Design School buildings at the University of Northumbria (right) are clad in a stainless steel mesh frame to reduce over-heating on sunny days.

THE GREAT NORTH MUSEUM: HANCOCK

This museum opened in 2009 following a £26m refurbishment. It houses premier collections which come from a variety of sources, including Newcastle University's Museum of Antiquities, the Natural History Society of Northumbria and the Society of Antiquaries of Newcastle upon Tyne. Highlights of this much-loved Victorian museum include a large-scale, interactive model of Hadrian's Wall, objects from the ancient Greeks and mummies from ancient Egypt, a planetarium, displays from the natural world and a life-size T-Rex dinosaur skeleton.

EARL GREY'S MONUMENT The man from whom Grey Street gets its name, prime minister Earl Grey, is celebrated in a monument sited at the top of Grainger Street. The twice life-size statue was sculpted in 1838 by Edward Hodges Bailey, who was also responsible for Nelson's statue in Trafalgar Square. In the 19th century there were lights on top of the monument which were lit in the event of an accident occurring in the city: red lights indicated fatalities; white lights meant that all the participants had survived. The low platform at the base of the monument is a popular meeting place for shoppers.

GREY STREET Built in 1836 by John Dobson and Richard Grainger, Grey Street has often been referred to as "England's finest street". Indeed the architectural style of the imposing Regency buildings that grace both sides of this gently curving thoroughfare is known as "Tyneside Classical". The heritage-led Grainger Town partnership has restored much of Newcastle city centre, including Grey Street, to its former glory; in the process more than 50 buildings which were on English Heritage's Buildings at Risk register have been rescued. The pavements have been upgraded too, using Caithness stone, Newcastle's original paving material. In recent years Newcastle has become one of the loveliest illuminated cities in the country. City centre streets have been enhanced at night by lighting, especially now that the beautiful stonework has been cleaned and its natural colours exposed. One example of this is the Theatre Royal; its distinctive portico has six massive Corinthian columns rising up from enormous moulded plinths supporting a classical triangular pediment bearing the

Royal Coat of Arms. The original Theatre Royal was located on Mosley Street; keen to incorporate a theatre into his newly designed city centre, Richard Grainger closed the old theatre and relocated it to Grey Street. The new theatre opened in February 1837.

CENTRAL STATION To many people the most beautiful feature of Central Station is the magnificent Victorian ironworked roofing with its majestic pillars and glass ceiling. The roof was unique at the time and won its designer, Charles Dobson, a prize at the Newcastle exhibition. The original six huge doors to the station, with their intricate iron latticework, still remain as does the first-class waiting room, now a popular bar and restaurant (left). Built between 1845 and 1850, the station and Neville Street, which was constructed at the same time, swept away a stretch of the 13th-century city wall. Just to the east of the booking hall stood the West Spital Tower. Countless citizens of Newcastle have walked under the portico to enter the station but this was a later addition built in 1863 to a design by Thomas Prosser. The station was opened by Queen Victoria in 1850; local legend has it that the monarch was not impressed when shown the bill!

CITY PANORAMA This view taken from the castle keep towards Newcastle's Moot Hall shows many of the major sights of both Newcastle and Gateshead through the ages, from the old city walls in the foreground to the Tyne Bridges and the new buildings of the Quayside in the distance. The city's 13th-century walls butt up against the Moot Hall now standing in the old courtyard of the castle, opposite the keep. William Stokoe designed the hall in 1810 in a Greek Doric and Pediment style. Further back, the 19th-century Swing Bridge is dominated by the 20th-century Tyne Bridge in the centre of the photograph. From the 21st century the "glass armadillo" of the Sage Gateshead on the far bank of the river and the curve of the Gateshead Millennium Bridge catch the eye.

ST JAMES' PARK The stadium (right), home of Newcastle FC, dominates the area just to the north of the city centre. The club, known as the Magpies – because of their distinctive black and white strip – have a loyal following in the city.

SALTWELL TOWERS Based in the heart of Gateshead, Saltwell Park is one of Britain's finest examples of a Victorian park. Opened to the public in 1876 when the park was bought for the people of the town by Gateshead Corporation, it is still known as "the people's park". Saltwell Park contains 11 listed buildings and monuments, including the magnificent Gothic mansion of Saltwell Towers and its gardens which were built between 1850 and 1862, one of two contrasting Victorian landscapes here. The other is the mid 19th-century parkland designed by Edward Kemp which consists of a series of gardens in different styles, from an open meadow to a formal Italianate garden.

GIBSIDE The Gibside Estate (left and right) was the property of the coal magnate George Bowes who developed this great "forest garden" over 200 years ago. It is now owned by the National Trust and offers the visitor 15 miles of woodland and walks beside the river Derwent with dramatic romantic ruins. This wonderful 18th-century forest garden is only three miles from the Metro Centre and visitors can enjoy the Octagonal and Lily Ponds, the Orangery and the Banqueting House, now a Landmark Trust property. Gibside Chapel was designed by James Paine and built as a mausoleum in the 1760s for George Bowes. Famous for its unusual three-tiered pulpit, it has today become a popular venue for weddings. The chapel was consecrated in 1812 and the mausoleum beneath the chapel is a plain circular vaulted chamber with a central column from which burial niches radiate around the walls. An avenue extends from the chapel to an obelisk with a statue of British Liberty, also designed by Paine in 1757.

JESMOND DENE A wooded valley which runs alongside the river Ouseburn between South Gosforth and Jesmond Vale, Jesmond Dene is rich in wildlife. Its exotic trees and shrubs, miles of footpaths and waterfalls provide a wonderful "green corridor" close to the heart of the city. It was formerly an industrialised valley that housed quarrying and ordnance testing. In 1835 William Armstrong, the famous industrialist, acquired the land partly to build a banqueting house to entertain his clients and also to develop Jesmond Dene House as a family home. Armstrong's philanthropy transformed the area from an industrial valley. By the 1870s Armstrong was spending much of his time at his new home at Cragside; in 1883 he donated the valley to the townspeople of Newcastle.

HOPPINGS The huge fairground called the Hoppings is best seen at night when tens of thousands of coloured lightbulbs burn brightly across the Town Moor. The Newcastle Hoppings is Europe's largest travelling fair and each year attracts hordes of visitors to the Moor in the last week of June. Local folklore has it that the rain that often accompanies the fair is the result of a Romany curse. The Temperance Fair held on the Town Moor was the forerunner of the Hoppings. There were children's games, sports and music and at the end of the day those gathered would feast and drink and then dance or "hop" around bonfires to the music of local pipers or fiddlers. These gatherings or fairs consequently became known as the "Hoppings".

ANGEL OF THE NORTH Constructed from sections transported to the site in 1998 and overlooking the A1, it is estimated that at least 90,000 motorists a day pass Antony Gormley's Angel of the North; it can also be seen clearly by rail passengers on the East Coast mainline from London to Edinburgh. Few realise the statue is actually hollow to allow for internal inspections with an access door on one of the shoulder blades, and that it is built on the site of a former colliery pit-head baths. It is taller than four double-decker buses and its wings are almost as long as those of a Jumbo jet. The Angel is made of weather resistant Cor-ten steel, containing a small amount of copper, which forms a patina on the surface that mellows with age; it contains enough steel to make four Chieftain tanks. In its exposed, hillside position, the statue has been designed to withstand winds of 100mph.

South Tyneside & Wearside

South Shields and Sunderland have fascinating histories and a range of attractions.

T he Marsden Rocks are sited on a beautiful stretch of coast just south of the mouth of the Tyne. This group of rocks is one of the most spectacular rock formations in Britain. Renowned for the thousands of pairs of seabirds that nest here, the shape of the group changed dramatically in 1996 when the arch that joined the present two stacks collapsed into the sea. The Marsden Rocks are reputedly haunted by the ghost of John the Jibber. He died a lingering death suspended in a bucket halfway down the cliff, having betrayed his fellow smugglers to the customs men.

SOUTER LIGHTHOUSE This distinctive red-and-white lighthouse is on the coast road in Whitburn. Built in 1871 it is now a fascinating museum of the life and workings of a Victorian lighthouse.

SOUTH SHIELDS TOWN HALL Officially opened in October 1910 with a peal of the five bells housed in its distinctive bell tower, South Shields town hall (right) was built to replace the old town built in 1768. It is sited in the middle of the market place.

LIFEBOAT MEMORIAL The South Shields Lifeboat Memorial is dedicated to the designers and crews of the early lifeboats; in 1829 the entire crew of 20 men were drowned when the town's lifeboat was lost. Willie Wouldhave designed the first self-righting lifeboat in 1789. The boat was lined with cork which made it almost impossible to capsize.

ARBEIA ROMAN FORT Four miles east of Hadrian's Wall this fort guarded the entrance to the river Tyne. Constructed around AD160 as a military supply depot for all of the 17 forts along the wall, the west gate of the fort has been reconstructed to house a museum.

HYLTON CASTLE This medieval gatehouse and tower in Hylton Dene, Sunderland stood guard over an important ferry crossing of the Wear. It is most famous for its ghost called the "Cauld Lad o' Hylton", a stable boy cruelly murdered by his master. The keep, four main walls and part of the chapel are all still standing. Over the years, the Castle and Dene had become neglected and vandalised. In 1992 a group of local residents set to work restoring the Dene and planning for its future. It is now in the care of English Heritage.

WASHINGTON OLD HALL The medieval house which once stood on the site of Washington Old Hall was, until the 13th century, the ancestral home of the family of George Washington, the first president of the United States. Today this picturesque stone manor house with its attractive gardens depicts the domestic life of a gentrified family just after the time of the English Civil War. The house was built in 1613 by Bishop James of Durham for his son. Used as a residence until the 19th century, the building was declared unfit for habitation in 1936. The house was restored thanks to a campaign led by local teacher Fred Hill, and in 1957 it passed into the ownership of the National Trust.

SUNDERLAND BRIDGE Built in 1929 the Wearmouth Bridge crosses the river Wear linking Sunderland with Hylton and Monkwearmouth on the north side of the river. When it was erected in 1796, the original bridge was the longest single-span cast-iron bridge in the world. The railway bridge behind was built in 1879 and extended the railway south from Monkwearmouth to the centre of Sunderland. In the mid 17th century the proximity of the Durham coalfield to the city necessitated new port facilities and an expansion in shipbuilding. By 1840 there were 65 shipyards on the river and Sunderland took its place as the biggest shipbuilding port in the world. The last coalmine, the Monkwearmouth Colliery, closed in 1993 and today is the site of the Stadium of Light, home to Sunderland FC. Sunderland was awarded city status in 1992. In recent years, Sunderland has undergone a renaissance in its quality of life. In addition to riverside walks and public art it now boasts a new marina complex that includes new housing and a watersports centre. Just upstream from the bridge is *Shadows in Another Light*, a sculpture (below left) in which the shadow cast by a tree represents a hammerhead crane unique to the Sunderland area.

SUNDERLAND CATHEDRAL Situated in the heart of the city, Sunderland Minster, St Michael's and All Angels, was originally a small medieval village church. The present church, however, is mainly 19th century with medieval fragments incorporated into the fabric. The building was inaugurated as the Minster for the City of Sunderland in January 1998.

ROKER LIGHTHOUSE AND MARINA

This distinctive red and white granite lighthouse stands at the end of the half-mile long Roker north pier where the river Wear discharges into the North Sea. The 75ft-conical tower was opened in 1903, the culmination of a giant project to build breakwaters on either side of the river mouth to create a sheltered harbour. Work began on the north pier in 1885. The first section of the pier was placed on top of a natural bedrock; further out a foundation of rubble and cement and giant concrete blocks were placed in position. Such was the difficulty and scale of the task that the first blocks were not laid in position until 1902, seventeen years after the work began. The 2,800ft north pier and lighthouse was finally completed in September 1903 and the south pier finished in 1912. The marina complex at the north dock is housed in a harbour originally constructed by Brunel in 1837. As well as pleasure boats, a small group of fishing vessels sail from the marina.

SUNDERLAND EMPIRE

With its distinctive tower topped off with a turreted dome and silver globe, this is a well-loved landmark in the city. The Empire's internal layout is virtually unique in theatre design since the side "slipper seats" almost border the stage. The foundation stone of the theatre was laid on September 29 1906 and in July 1907 the Edwardian music hall favourite Vesta Tilley declared the Empire open when performing on stage. The theatre was originally called the Empire Palace and on opening it had a 3,000-seat auditorium. Legendary comedy stars Stan Laurel and Charlie Chaplin performed here; tragically, on the opening night of *The Mating Season* in 1976, the actor Sid James of *Carry On* fame died on stage after suffering a heart attack. In 2004 the Empire re-opened after a £4.5m refit.

SUNDERLAND WINTER GARDENS

This spectacular building houses a superb botanical collection of over 1,500 plants of 146 species in naturalistic settings under a single-span 98.5ft (30m) dome. The gardens display samples of many important plants from around the world and visitors can take a staircase or scenic lift up to a treetop walkway where they can look down into an amazing rainforest canopy below. The gardens also house a number of exotic palms from countries such as Australia, Madagascar and Malaysia. The Winter Gardens are linked to Sunderland's remodelled museum and the upgraded and re-landscaped Mowbray Park. Visitors enter the museum via a striking new glazed entrance which leads into the "museum street".

PENSHAW MONUMENT Built in 1844 by private subscription and designed by John and Benjamin Green of Newcastle, the Penshaw Monument is unusual in that it has no inscription. Built in the form of a 100ft (30.5m) long, 50ft (15m) wide and 70ft (21m) high ruined Greek temple, the monument is based on the Thesion, the Temple of Theseus in Athens. It commemorates John George Lambton, first Earl of Durham (known as Radical Jack). Located opposite Herrington Country Park, its high position astride Penshaw Hill gives views as far afield as Durham Cathedral and the north Pennines. Local folklore has it that the legendary Lambton Worm, a fearsome dragon, wound itself 10 times around Penshaw Hill.

FULWELL MILL A unique Sunderland landmark, Fulwell Mill is the only working windmill in north-east England. It was built in 1821 and has recently been restored. Visitors can enjoy demonstrations of the ancient art of cornmilling and get an insight into the life of the workings of a 19th-century windmill.

GLASS CENTRE Set on the north bank of the river Wear, the award-winning National Glass Centre is a stunning building and acts as a base for artists, designers and makers to meet and create new products and artworks. The University of Sunderland's Glass, Architectural Glass and Ceramics Departments are located in the centre as is the International Institute for Research in Glass.

UNIVERSITY OF SUNDERLAND
Sunderland University has two main sites within the city. Perched on the north bank of the river Wear, the Sir Tom Cowie Campus at St Peter's houses the Sunderland Business School, the impressive David Goldman Informatics Centre and the Media Centre. St Peter's Campus has several modern buildings arranged around a large open plaza, called University Square.

Durham

This ancient city with its world-famous castle and cathedral is perched dramatically on a loop of the river Wear.

Durham is one of the most attractive cities in Britain. Modern and ancient buildings, including the world famous castle and cathedral, are jammed together on a narrow site created as the river Wear flows in a hairpin bend, almost encircling a huge outcrop of sandstone on which the town is built. It is little wonder that this collection of historic buildings has been designated as a World Heritage Site. But the county of Durham is more than the city which bears its name. It contains pretty fortified towns and castles including Raby, Brancepeth and Barnard Castle, outstanding museums such as those at Beamish and Bowes, ecclesiastical ruins including those at Egglestone Abbey and elegant towns such as Bishop Auckland. The roots of Christianity in Britain go deep in County Durham – monks from Holy Island sought shelter in the towns and cities of the area and helped establish them as important religious settlements. The remains of the Venerable Bede and St Cuthbert are interred at Durham Cathedral.

DURHAM CATHEDRAL Begun by Bishop William of Calais in 1093, Durham Cathedral is an outstanding example of Romanesque architecture. Inside the cathedral, the nave is particularly striking with its massive spiral and zig-zag decorated columns and the larger multiple-columned compound piers which support the impressive diamond-ribbed vaulting of the ceiling high above. The cathedral has been a centre for pilgrimage throughout its 900-year history. It contains the tombs of St Cuthbert, the saintly seventh-century bishop of Lindisfarne and that of the Venerable Bede, the first English historian, which were placed there in 1370. There have been occasions over the centuries when the cathedral has suffered

damage and vandalism. The 14th-century altar screen originally contained 107 alabaster figures but many were vandalised in the 16th century. In 1650 further damage was caused when Cromwell imprisoned 4,000 Scots in the cathedral. One of its most beautiful features today is the huge rose window with its central core depicting Christ surrounded by the apostles; it was created in the 15th century and reconstructed in the 18th. The cloisters adjoin the south side of the cathedral and are clustered around a small square green known as the Cloister Garth. The four covered cloister walkways were designed so that monks would have shelter when relaxing, studying and praying. The walkway on the northern side of the cloisters by the main cathedral wall was formerly the monk's scriptorium and contained reading chambers for study. The buildings surrounding the Cloister Garth included the refectory, the chapter house, the monk's dormitory and the kitchen.

DURHAM CASTLE A fine example of the Norman motte and bailey style of fortification, the building of Durham Castle began in 1072 with a circular keep on top of the hill overlooking the town. This was part of William the Conqueror's plan to pacify the region; the castle was enlarged in 1174. During the middle ages, Durham was one of a number of castles spread throughout the north to counter the threat of invasion from the Scots. Later it was taken over as the principal residence of the Bishops of Durham or the Prince Bishops as they were known, since they administered the county on behalf of the Crown. It was they who built the magnificent halls and chapel, rare survivors of secular Norman splendour. The medieval bishops continued to develop the castle and in the 17th century yet more lavish accommodation was provided. In the 1830s the bishops left the castle and it became part of the University of Durham.

THE GATEHOUSE, DURHAM CASTLE
The castle court is entered from the Green by the main Gatehouse, in front of which is the site of the barbican and moat. To the west of the Gatehouse is the Great Hall, probably built by Bishop Anthony Bek (1284-1311) in the 13th and 14th centuries and now used as the dining hall of the university – serving much the same purpose as was originally intended. The basement of the hall now houses wine cellars. Opposite the Gatehouse is one of the oldest parts of the castle, built by Bishop Pudsey (1153-1195). The keep at Durham Castle is not original but is a well-constructed Victorian replica built to the original plans.

DURHAM MARKET PLACE

Durham's cobbled Market Place, site of the town hall and Guildhall, has medieval origins but the present Market Square is largely of Victorian origin. In the summer visitors can often enjoy street entertainment set amongst the stunning floral displays. Built in 1858, the spire of the Church of St Nicholas dominates the eastern side of the Market Place. The Victorian church of St Nicholas replaced a medieval church which dated from the early part of the 12th century. Unlike the present church this building had a tower rather than a spire. Today much of Durham's shopping area is closed to modern traffic, making for a relaxed atmosphere. The city is very compact yet still offers a wide range of facilities to the visitor and a variety of shops and restaurants co-exist happily with the Victorian market.

PREBENDS BRIDGE A stroll along the Durham Riverbanks is a must for any visitor to the city. The best view of Durham Cathedral, with its western towers soaring majestically above the wooded river bank, is from Prebends Bridge, which was built in 1777. The bridge formed a major part of the Durham Riverbanks Gardens which surrounded the peninsula from the 16th to the 18th centuries, and today it also offers fine views of the weir and Fulling Mill, now part of the university. There are three other ancient monuments within the Riverbanks area – Elvet Bridge, the Water Gate and Framwellgate Bridge.

BRANCEPETH CASTLE Built in the 11th century, Brancepeth Castle was originally the home of a Saxon lord; it eventually became the property of the Nevilles until confiscated by Elizabeth I. Sir Henry Bellaysyse, who owned the castle in the early 18th century had a daughter, Mary, who became attracted to a local man, Bobby Shaftoe. Her love for Bobby became the subject of the famous song. In 1796 William Russell, a broker from Sunderland, bought the castle; his son Matthew, who re-built the castle, owned numerous coalmines in the area and was alleged to be the richest commoner in England. The poet Tennyson was a regular visitor during the 19th century and the castle continued to be occupied until the First World War.

BRANCEPETH VILLAGE Brancepeth is a quiet attractive village distinguished by the creeper-covered cottages leading up to the castle gates. Old-fashioned street lights line the streets and there is an ancient bench taken from the old railway station that once stood on the outskirts of the village. The first-recorded village rector was a monk from Durham called Haeming who has left a signature dating back to 1085. Alfred, Lord Tennyson, Poet Laureate from 1850 to 1892, wrote his famous Victorian poem *Maud* at Brancepeth.

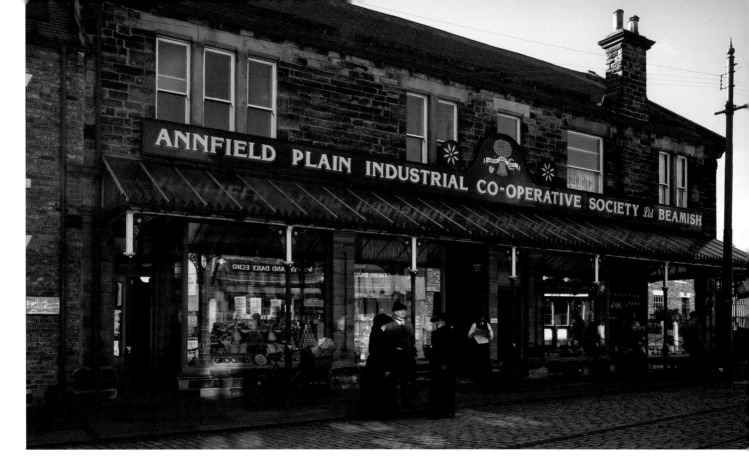

BEAMISH OPEN AIR MUSEUM The world-famous open air museum at Beamish was set up in 1970 and tells the story of the people of the north-east of England at two important points of their history – in 1825 and 1913. The museum is made up of old buildings from the region. Some, such as the Drift Mine, Home Farm and Pockerley Manor were already on the site; others have been brought from their original location and carefully reconstructed. There are no labels or glass cases at Beamish; the idea is to give visitors a realistic view of life in the past. Staff are dressed in costume and the feeling is much more of being part of a theatrical production than walking through the aisles of a traditional museum.

BISHOP AUCKLAND The attractive town of Bishop Auckland is situated at the confluence of the river Wear and the river Gaunless; it has been the site of an important market since medieval times. As its name implies, the town has been the seat of the Bishops of Durham since the 12th century. Bishop Auckland grew up around the gates of Auckland Castle which is still the official residence of the Bishops of Durham. Originally a Norman manor house and hunting lodge, today the castle stands in its own park east of the town's marketplace. The French-style town hall situated in the marketplace is a Grade I listed building. The main street in Bishop Auckland follows the course of the Roman Dere Street which led to the Roman fort of Binchester, just to the north of the town.

BISHOP'S PALACE Auckland Castle has been the home of the Bishops of Durham – the "Bishop's Palace" – for over 800 years. Dating from the 12th century it was originally a banqueting hall and hunting lodge and was gradually developed for the Prince Bishops into one of the most ornate palaces in Britain. The magnificent chapel is believed to be the largest private place of worship in Europe. Although the Prince Bishops had a number of other residences, the castle seems to have been their favourite and in 1832 it became their official home.

RABY CASTLE One of the largest and most impressive of England's medieval castles, Raby is famous for its beautiful walled gardens and deer park. King Canute owned the estate in the early 11th century and may well have built the first castle here. The present building was begun by John, 3rd Baron Nevill in about 1360. The castle is in an excellent state of preservation and includes a sturdy gatehouse, complete with portcullis and "murder holes" for pouring oil on attackers. At the south-east corner of the castle is the Bulmer's Tower, almost unique in castle architecture since it has five sides. The castle has a cavernous kitchen built in 1360 and a garrison room with walls between 10 and 20ft thick. In 1569, 700 knights gathered in the medieval baron's hall to plot the doomed "Rising of the North" in support of Mary, Queen of Scots against Elizabeth I. In the 1840s the sumptuously furnished Octagon drawing room was added.

STAINDROP One of County Durham's most fascinating villages, Staindrop, just south of Raby Castle, mainly consists of 18th-century stone houses surrounding a series of interlocking greens which are lined with limes and horse chestnuts. The main street is an attractive mix of stone cottages, some brightly painted, with the square steeple of St Mary's church dominating the view. The side roads still have signs of the many old workshops and stables that demonstrate the wealth of the village in the 18th and 19th centuries. In 1971 the centre of the village was designated a conservation area in order to protect its unique environment.

BARNARD CASTLE Perched high on top of a steep bank overlooking the river Tees, Barnard Castle was first built around the year 1095 and later fortifed again by Bernard Baliol in 1135. The castle gave its name to the town that grew up alongside it. Amongst later owners were the Prince Bishops and Richard III. The castle played an important part in the defeat of the northern Earls who rose against Elizabeth in 1569. The site was badly damaged in 1630 when Sir Henry Vane bought it in order to use its stone to rebuild his home at Raby Castle. The town itself has a unique character and is recognised nationally as one of the most architecturally important towns in the United Kingdom. The Market Cross and the 12th-century Church of St Mary are both fine features. The town is full of fascinating old shops and is a wonderful centre for antique collectors. Charles Dickens stayed at The King's Head when researching his novel *Nicholas Nickleby*.

BOWES MUSEUM This famous museum in Barnard Castle originated in a private foundation created between 1862 and 1875 by John and Josephine Bowes. It was conceived and purpose-built as a public art gallery by the French architect Jules Pellechet and opened in 1892. The building is designed in the style of a French chateau and has public galleries on three floors and a collection of European fine and decorative arts from the middle ages to early Victorian times. There is particular emphasis on the arts of France including items from the Bowes' home in Paris. Perhaps the best known exhibit in the museum is the famous Silver Swan, a life-size musical automaton which consists of a clockwork mechanism covered in silver plumage above a music box. In the 40 seconds of musical movement the swan turns its head to the left and right and appears to preen its back. It then spots a fish, bends down, catches and swallows its prey. As the music stops the swan resumes its upright position. The Bowes Museum, housed in a typically French grand chateau, puts the visitor in mind of grand houses in the French countryside. It has some of the best collections of European art in Britain. French, Spanish and Italian paintings are a feature of the collection together with European ceramics and textiles. The museum also houses collections of archaeological finds from County Durham and artefacts showing the social history of Teesside.

EGGLESTONE ABBEY The ruins of Egglestone Abbey perch above a steep slope overlooking the river Tees just south of Barnard Castle. The abbey lies in the grounds of Egglestone Hall which has old walled gardens, winding paths and lawns as well as many rare plants and shrubs. It was founded in 1195 but was not wealthy compared to many other monastic houses and at times had problems maintaining the required number of brethren to retain its status as an abbey. The abbey also had to contend with regular raids by the Scots. After the Dissolution, the land was granted to Robert Streely in 1548. Like many Tudor land-owners, he turned it into a presti-gious house and this is apparent in the ruins today. In the 19th century much of the abbey was pulled down and some of the stonework was re-used to pave the stable yard at nearby Rokeby Hall.

KILLHOPE The Killhope lead-mining museum in Upper Weardale is a reconstructed mine powered by a water wheel, typical of the many leadmines operating in the north Pennines during the 19th century. The museum allows visitors to go underground and experience the working lives of the miners. The Park Level mine at Killhope was opened in 1853 and for a few short years in the 1870s the mine was one of the richest in the whole of Britain. It ceased working around 1911 but reopened for a short while during the First World War. Park Level Mill with its giant waterwheel was built in the late 1870s to help separate out the lead ore from waste. Today it is the only wheel that survives in the area.

ROOKHOPE Rookhope lies snugly in the upper reaches of the Rookhope Burn and it is here that the earliest references to mineral mining in this area are recorded. In 1153 King Stephen granted a licence for an iron mine and a lead mine in "Rychup". By the late 18th century the whole area was covered with smelting mills and littered with the distinctive giant chimneys and brick flues that helped carry the poisonous gases away from the workplaces. Outside the village on the road to Allenheads is "Rookhope Arch", the one remaining arch of a bridge that carried a two-mile long twin flue linked to the nearby smelt-mill. The roads to the village are very narrow but there are superb views across the north Pennines. On December 8th 1569, the valley was the setting for a border battle in which a large group of mosstroopers (cattle raiders) were caught after they had stolen a herd of cattle from Weardale. The event is remembered in the local ballad *The Rookhope Ryde*.

STANHOPE HALL The little market town of Stanhope, with its cobbled marketplace, lies 20 miles (30km) west of the city of Durham. In the middle ages, the Prince Bishops would hold "forest courts" in the town for locals accused of poaching. Just outside the village is Stanhope Hall, an attractive building which was the ancestral home of the Fetherstonhalgh family until the last male of the family was killed in the Civil War. William de Monte lived here in the middle of the 12th century in the reign of King Stephen.

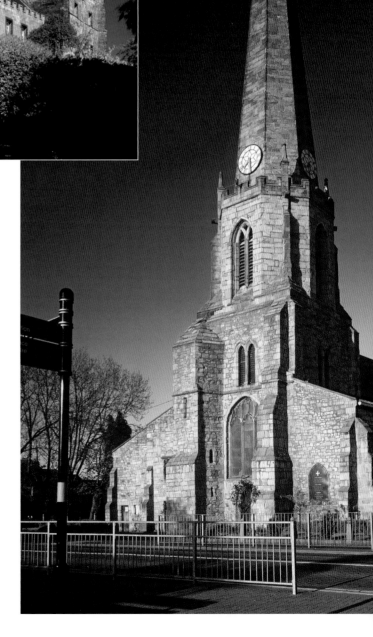

LUMLEY CASTLE This magnificent building is set within nine acres of parkland, overlooking the river Wear and situated near Chester-le-Street. It was built in 1392 as a manor house and was later converted by Sir Ralph Lumley to the castle that can be seen today. Sir Ralph built four great corner towers and the intervening buildings as well as the main gateway. Local legend has it that Lumley is haunted by Lily Lumley, a 14th-century lady of the manor and wife of Sir Ralph, who was apparently thrown down a well by two priests after she refused to convert to Catholicism when her husband was absent as Governor of Berwick. In the 18th century the basement of the south-west tower was altered by Sir John Vanbrugh, the architect of Blenheim Palace and Seaton Delaval Hall in Northumberland. Today the castle is a hotel.

ST MARY'S, CHESTER-LE-STREET The Parish Church of Saint Mary and Saint Cuthbert is one of the oldest churches in the north of England, and contains a facsimile of the Lindisfarne Gospels, presented in 2005. The town's place in history is assured – the Romans had a fort here in AD122 which they called *Congangium*, and it was in the town that the Bible was first translated into English. There has been a Christian community at Chester-le-Street since 883. In this year, monks from the abbey of Lindisfarne were fleeing Viking raids and carrying the body of Saint Cuthbert. Sheltering at Chester-le-Street they built a shrine which became, for more than a century, the Cathedral of the Kingdom of Northumbria. In 999 the monks took the coffin to Durham where it still lies in Durham Cathedral. Today the town has a thriving outdoor market which is held weekly every Tuesday, Friday and Saturday; it is also the home of Durham County Cricket Club and has one of the most attractive county cricket grounds in the country.

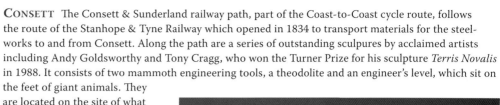

CONSETT The Consett & Sunderland railway path, part of the Coast-to-Coast cycle route, follows the route of the Stanhope & Tyne Railway which opened in 1834 to transport materials for the steelworks to and from Consett. Along the path are a series of outstanding sculpures by acclaimed artists including Andy Goldsworthy and Tony Cragg, who won the Turner Prize for his sculpture *Terris Novalis* in 1988. It consists of two mammoth engineering tools, a theodolite and an engineer's level, which sit on

the feet of giant animals. They are located on the site of what was once the largest steelworks in Europe and symbolise the economic regeneration of the Consett area. The original iron-works were set up in 1840 on what was a bleak moorland hillside and as they grew the town of Consett developed beside them. In 1980 the Consett Steelworks closed causing a devastating blow to the town and community. Today Consett has become a centre for business and retail serving the surrounding countryside and is the administrative centre for Derwentside council.

CAUSEY ARCH Spanning almost 90ft (27m) of the Causey Burn gorge and towering 80ft (24m) above it, Causey Arch was designed by Ralph Wood and built between 1725-6; it is recognised as the oldest surviving single arch railway bridge in the world. Wood is reputed to have used Roman technology to construct the bridge, making use of the steep sides of the valley to hold up the arch. The bridge was constructed to provide a link for coal transportation between Tanfield and the river Tyne. Now one of the principal attractions in the Causey Country Park, it was restored and waterproofed by Durham County Council in 1981. Nearby is the Tanfield Railway, which is claimed to be the world's oldest operating railway; opened in 1725 it ran commercially until 1962 and is now run by volunteers. Originally horses hauled small wagons along wooden tracks but these were replaced in the 19th century by metal rails and locomotives.

Tees Valley

One of the hidden beauty spots of north-east England, the Tees Valley has wild moorlands, fast-flowing rivers and historic towns.

The river Tees rises in the foothills of the north Pennines and flows east to meet the sea at Teesmouth, south of Hartlepool. The Upper Tees valley is characterised by its heather-clad moorland and rolling farmland interspersed with the scattered ruins of the area's industrial past – in particular leadmining. This upland area is rich in nationally renowned beauty spots which include the dramatic waterfalls at High Force and Cauldron Spout. The river then flows past historic towns and villages which include Middleton-in-Teesdale and Darlington; in its final stretches it passes through towns and cities such as Stockton-on-Tees, Middlesbrough and Hartlepool which form the industrial heartland of the region. Although lower Teesside has a reputation as an area dominated by heavy industry and manufacturing, its beautiful countryside and regenerated urban areas make for an attractive and dynamic environment.

HIGH FORCE At 70ft (21m) this is the highest unbroken waterfall in England. After a period of heavy rain the roaring boom of the falls can be heard from a distance. There are two other waterfalls on this stretch of the river Tees – Low Force is about one mile downstream, whilst Cauldron Force lies four miles upstream. Cauldron Spout is the highest waterfall in England. The thunderous cascade drops 200ft (61m) down a 450ft (137m) long series of steps.

HOLWICK SCAR Four miles to the north-west of Middleton-in-Teesdale lies the magnificent escarpment of volcanic rock known as Holwick Scar. Part of the Great Whin Sill, the Scar faces north-east across upper Teesdale near the village of Holwick. This massive structure is often thought to look like an ancient stone castle as the nature of the crags is reminiscent of circular stone towers. The Scar forms part of a group of crags in Upper Teesdale, the others being Falcon Clints, Cronkley Scar, Raven Scar and Dineholm Scar. These crags are famous both for rare breeding birds such as peregrine falcon, raven and ring ouzel and their equally rare and fragile plant life – indeed some of the plant communities are specially protected under British and international legislation. They include trees, lichen and ferns; one of these plants is a microspecies of hawkweed only known in Upper Teesdale and not found anywhere else in the world.

MIDDLETON-IN-TEESDALE The Tees flows gently through the upper reaches of Teesdale some two miles north of High Force. At this point the river flows through villages that are rich in history. The largest of these is Middleton-in-Teesdale where in the 1880s the London Lead Company established its northern headquarters. The impact of this can still be seen in the many buildings that symbolise Victorian prosperity. The village is known to have existed since the time of the Norsemen when King Canute owned the land.

LOW FORCE This attractive set of waterfalls is in upper Teesside, three miles north-west of Middleton-on-Tees. Many visitors prefer to visit this set of falls rather than those of High Force or Cauldron Spout higher up the river because of the ease of access and the pretty riverside walks alongside the falls. Just below Low Force is Winch (or Wynch) bridge – a cast-iron and wooden suspension footbridge which was built in the middle of the 18th century to transport Holwick leadminers to the leadmine at Little Eggleshope in the fells to the north of the river. The name "force" comes from a Norse word meaning a waterfall. Close by is the Bowless visitor centre housed in an old Methodist chapel and run by Durham Wildlife Trust. The visitor centre has exhibitions of local fauna and wildlife and a wealth of information about walking in the area.

DARLINGTON The clock that towers over Darlington is part of the former Town Hall building. Darlington is well-known for its parks and leafy suburbs and despite its long history, dating from Saxon times, the town centre mostly consists of Victorian and 20th-century buildings. A sublime exception is the 12th-century Church of St Cuthbert, which stands on the banks of the river Skerne; it was built by Hugh Pudsey, one of the Prince Bishops of Durham, and is sometimes referred to as the "Lady of the North". Darlington owes much of its growth to the great Quaker families who lived here in the 18th and 19th centuries. It is famed worldwide as the birthplace of the railways. The world's first public railway opened here on September 27 1825; as well as carrying coal to Stockton, the train had room for 600 passengers. Today Darlington's railway history is celebrated by a brick sculpture. Created in 1997 by David Mach, the sculpture contains 185,000 bricks and weighs 15,000 tonnes. It is modelled on the famous *Mallard*, the 1938 steam locomotive that reached a speed of 126mph, and was the long-time holder of the world rail-speed record.

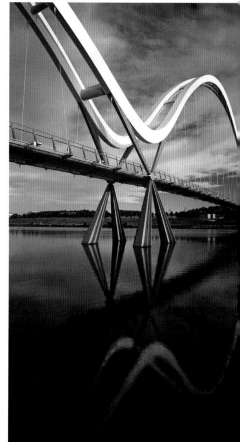

STOCKTON-ON-TEES The lights of Stockton's Teesquay Millennium Footbridge reflect on the waters of the river as the sun sets slowly behind. Stockton can trace its origins back to Saxon times whilst its market is first recorded as being held in 1310. The town is well known for its railway connections; it also made another tremendous impact on the history of the world when in 1826 John Walker invented the friction match. The great comic and music hall entertainer Will Hay was born in Stockton and the famous Conservative politician and prime minister, Harold Macmillan, the Earl of Stockton, represented the town as its MP for many years. The Tees Barrage has created a stretch of clean, high-quality deep water making the river Tees suitable for water-sports including sailing, rowing, wind-surfing, water-skiing, kayaking and canoeing. A man-made white-water course can also be found on the Tees. A footbridge and cycleway have been built which allows the public to view the structure of the barrage from close quarters and also enjoy riverside walks and cycling along its banks.

MIDDLESBROUGH In the shadow of the famous Transporter Bridge, Middlesbrough's dockland landscape has been the subject of recent redevelopment. Seen here is Anish Kapoor's *Temenos* – Britain's largest sculpture, it is as tall as Nelson's Column. The sculpture – a series of giant hoops and wires which float above the dockland area – was formally "unveiled" in June 2010. It is the first in a planned series of five giant sculptures to be installed in the Tees Valley over the next decade. Today Middlesbrough Town Hall (below right) is a popular musical venue hosting everything from international orchestras to world famous rock bands. Like the other cities of the north-east, Middlesbrough has invested in public art as part of its rejuvenation – containing fibre optics and mirrors, the 33ft (10m) high interactive stainless-steel obelisk at Binns Corner is a good example.

CLOCK TOWER This distinctive redbrick tower situated on the south bank of the river Tees was built by John Middleton in 1870 as both a clock tower and a reservoir to maintain water pressure to power dock cranes and dockside gates.

BOTTLE OF NOTES SCULPTURE This iconic sculpture sits next to the Institute of Art.

WILF MANNION STATUE One of the town's most famous players at the Riverside stadium.

MIDDLESBROUGH INDUSTRY In 1801 Middlesbrough was no more than a small farmstead occupied by about a dozen people. The farm and surrounding land was bought by a group of Quaker businessmen from Darlington who set about building a port to export coal and other commodities; from these beginnings, the town of Middlesbrough was born. The mid 19th century saw Middlesbrough's population grow exponentially – from 40 people in 1829 to 7,600 by 1851. In this year the discovery of iron ore in the Cleveland Hills prompted local businessmen to build Teesside's first blast furnace in the town. A mere nine years later the population had increased to 20,000. The Tees Transporter Bridge, shown here, connects Middlesbrough on the south bank of the Tees to Port Clarence on the north bank. The gondola suspended beneath the bridge travels from one bank to the other in 90 seconds. Newport Bridge – the first vertical lift bridge in Britain– was built so that the central section can be raised to allow ships to pass beneath. Opened by the Duke of York in 1934 its lifting mechanism allows the road to be raised 100ft (30.5m) in one and a half minutes.

HARTLEPOOL The magnificent Abbey Church of St Hilda dominates the approach by sea and land to the Hartlepool headland and nearby the old town walls of Hartlepool, completed in 1333, can still be seen. Mainly Early English, dating from 1185, St Hilda's is on the site of an abbey which flourished as early as 658. Until the second quarter of the 19th century, Hartlepool was a collection of small, isolated villages, sand dunes and marshes. By the end of the century, however, it had become the fifth largest shipping port in the United Kingdom. Hartlepool was a target for enemy firepower during the First World War. On the morning of December 16 1914 the German navy bombarded the town for 35 minutes, resulting in the deaths of 117 townsfolk. The bustling Hartlepool Marina is one of the major signs of the successful regeneration of the town. The new marina has become an

the triple masts of HMS *Trincomalee*. Built of teak in India in 1817 she is the oldest fighting ship still afloat in the country. This beautiful sailing ship was first moored in West Hartlepool in 1862 and was used as a training ship for young recruits to the navy. In 1897 the *Trincomalee* was sold for scrap but she was rescued, repaired and once again became a training vessel in 1903. She saw service during the Second World War.

HARTLEPOOL MONKEY During the Napoleonic Wars there was an almost irrational fear amongst the British population of imminent invasion and of French spies. When a pet monkey was washed ashore from a French ship wrecked off the Hartlepool coast, local fisherman immediately put the animal on trial and came to the conclusion that the monkey was a French spy. The unfortunate monkey was hanged from the mast of a local ship. A statue commemorating this event stands near the lock gates of the marina. Hartlepool United FC has a monkey as a mascot because of this historic event.

attractive focal point with waterside restaurants and promenades. The marina is not restricted to pleasure craft and many working boats of differing sizes can be seen scattered around the piers. In the centre of the marina is the award-winning Historic Quay, a reproduction of an 18th-century seaport portraying sights, sounds and smells of sealife at the time. Dominating the marina area are

TALL SHIPS RACE Races for sail training ships –often known as "tall ships" – are held all around the world and are designed to encourage international friendship and training for young people in the art of sailing. The 2010 race began in Antwerp and ended in Hartlepool having called en route to Aalborg in Denmark and Kristiansand in Norway. One hundred tall ships took part in the race and this maritime spectacular meant that the Victoria harbour was transformed into a maritime village for the four days when ships ended the race. On the 10th August the ships ceremoniously paraded out of Hartlepool Quays, along the coast in a "Parade of Sail" and made their way back to their home ports.

SALTBURN The beach at Saltburn is a popular venue for surfing and is famous for its attractive walks. Saltburn was once a fashionable resort for the Victorians with its own rail link and formal gardens. A miniature railway which still exists was constructed at around the same time. Just behind the seafront an Italianate garden and an ancient wooded area called Rifts Wood make up the Saltburn Valley gardens; they merge with a nature reserve and offer the visitor a superb display of both ornamental plants and wildflowers. The town and beach were once a hotbed of smuggling and many reminders of this activity can still be seen in Saltburn. Saltburn Pier is the only remaining pier on the north-east coast and is now practically half its original length due to the pounding of the sea over the years. Completed in 1869 the pier was originally 1,400ft (427m) long; after restoration it was reopened in 1978 at its present length of 681ft (208m). It was however still in need of repair and further restoration work was completed in 2001. Saltburn Pier can be reached from the town by the cliff lift which was opened in 1884.

ROSEBERRY TOPPING Roseberry Topping is one of the most distinctively-shaped hills in the country. Often referred to by locals as the "Matterhorn of Cleveland", its high summit is a popular tourist attraction as it provides excellent 360 degree views of the region. On a clear day it is possible to see as far as Teesside in one direction and the Yorkshire Dales in another. Also known as Odin's Hill, "Topping", from *toppen* is one of a number of old Norse words for a hill. Roseberry Topping is shaped rather like the breaking crest of a wave, thanks to a mining accident. In 1880 iron ore began to be mined by a local company to supply the foundries of nearby Middlesbrough. Mining stopped in 1920 but the following year a huge landslide occurred that created the hill's distinctive shape; it is thought that the collapse of the mineworkings caused this. Now in the care of the National Trust, a spur of the Cleveland Way footpath runs up to the summit.

COOK MONUMENT

Directly south of Roseberry Topping and south-east of the village of Great Ayton stands a distinctive monument to Captain Cook. This tall, stone-built structure is linked with Roseberry Topping by the Cleveland Way long-distance footpath; it can be reached easily from the car park at Gribdale Gate. The monument was erected in 1827 by Robert Campion of Whitby; it lies a few miles from Marton to the north-west where the famous explorer was born,

and it overlooks Great Ayton where he attended the village school between 1736 and 1740. The school was originally founded as a charity school by Michael Postgate, a local landowner; it has now been converted into the Captain Cook Schoolroom Museum. From here there are panoramic views across to Roseberry Topping and along the curve of the Cleveland Hills. The Captain Cook Birthplace Museum opened in 1978, the 250th anniversary of Cook's birth. It stands close to the granite urn marking the spot where he was born in Stewart Park, Marton.

GUISBOROUGH PRIORY

Founded by Robert de Brus in 1119, Guisborough Priory was home to Augustinian monks. Robert was an ancestor of Robert the Bruce, whose father is buried here. The large church was destroyed by Henry VIII during the reformation but the huge east gable wall still stands and is an outstanding example of Gothic architecture showing the wealth of the priory. It was built immediately after a disastrous fire of 1289 and survived because it was used as a folly by some of the later owners. The 12th-century gatehouse still exists; it was the original entrance and is the oldest part of the priory still standing. Like other religious houses in the north the priory suffered from periodic raids by the Scots.

The publishers would like to thank English Heritage and the National Trust for the opportunity in this book to showcase some of the richest natural and built heritage to be found in north-east England.

First published in 2011 by Myriad Books Limited
35 Bishopsthorpe Road
London SE26 4PA

Photographs and text copyright ©
2011 Graeme Peacock

ISBN   1 84746 388 6
EAN 978 1 84746 388 3

Designed by Jerry Goldie Graphic Design

Printed in China

www.myriadbooks.com